More Stories From A Trepid Sailor

Sailing the Inside Passage Seattle to Alaska

Jacquelyn Watt
11/20/2012

A collection of true stories that highlight the adventures and excitement of mariners sailing the waters of the Inside Passage, Seattle to Glacier Bay Alaska .Meet the 40 foot SV-Shadowfax, Captain Bob and his First Mate, wife Jacquelyn, who was the chronicler of their voyage.

Copyright © 2012 by Mary Jacquelyn Watt. (Lulu author)

ISBN 978-1-300-13317-9

1

Contents

This book is dedicated to our grandchildren…

Tor

Anabelle

Alex

and

Max,

to their cousins **Shannon, Kyle** and **Maddie**

and , of course,**Raymond**

With Love

My Bags Are Packed

April 30, 2008 Meydenbauer Bay, Bellevue ,Wa, USA

"My bags are packed, I'm ready to go"…or so the song goes, and our bags are <u>ready</u>!
The Shadowfax is well prepared for its 2008 journey up the Inside Passage from Seattle to Alaska for the second time. Our plan is to leave the dock at Meydenbauer Bay in Bellevue on May 1, tomorrow.

We were tormented onboard by voltage regulator and electrical gremlins on our 2006 trip. Now in 2008 we have a NEW alternator, NEW voltage regulator and two 75 watt solar panels for power augmentation. We also have a new Canadian courtesy flag to replace the prior flag which beaten and shredded by the winds of the Inside Passage. The canvas covering the cockpit has been repaired and re-sewn as it suffered from the winds as well or perhaps it was the voracious biting horseflies that did the damage. It is one day prior to the departure date and my stomach is already clenched with anticipation and some fear. I am calming myself with the knowledge that I have packed my favorite purple fleece bathrobe and favorite down coat to cocoon and comfort me as we start off in this unusually chilly spring. This will augment the cases of cocoa stowed on board for succor during the trip.

I have vacillated between taking a blanket throw or the down sleeping bag capable of withstanding (and did) the frigid summit climb of Mount Rainier. Captain Bob has nixed the sleeping bag idea, so throw blanket it will be. It has occurred to me to chart my fear from a scale of one to ten, as one reports pain to a nurse after surgery. This is not necessary just a fear of cold, but of a healthy respect and fear of these Pacific Northwest waters we sail. This fear started for me as a child when a grandparent attempted to take the whole family on a private "cruise" in the straits of Juan de Fuca. This voyage was taken in complete disregard of tides and gale warnings, in an old fifty foot wood fishing boat. The vessel had been converted to a pleasure craft, but still retained the ancient diesel engine that propelled the boat a knot or two less than the tidal flow of the region. Faced with incoming tides, over 20 foot waves and strong winds the boat proved incapable of forward motion and was swept (by now in the dark) with captain and family from the middle of the Straits completely through the San Juan Islands to Sucia Island. Reefs and rocks were miraculously avoided and when morning dawned my grandparent was not sure where the vessel had managed to drop anchor. During this whole episode my grandparent had taken the prudent move of locking all the children, I think there were 7 or 8 of us, in the old fishing hold where we were flung from side to side for the whole night crying and seasick in the dark, fearing the boat would sink with us incarcerated inside. This left an indelible impression on all of us.

Today my level is 6, even though I am comfortably snuggled in my bed, warm, motionless, the only sounds the far off traffic in Bellevue. Tomorrow we leave and go back to motion, sounds of engine, and the whistling of wind in the rigging.

Alaska here we come!

Nine Ton Ballerina

May 2, 2008 Saratoga Passage, Camano Island,Wa.

The first 12 hours of our voyage was spent traveling
through the locks, motoring to Hat Island and then
backtracking to Everett for the night. We had successfully
reached our destination and managed to come within 50
feet of the Hat Island docks when the low tide and the
constantly encroaching sands conspired to stop us. The
keel of the Shadowfax hesitantly slid into the shallow mud
of the Hat Island Marina, the grounding so gentle it was
barely perceptible, except that our slight forward coasting
motion abruptly halted. A quick backing maneuver and we
were freed, unable to reach our intended destination for the
evening. It was tempting to attempt entry at a different
angle, but reason prevailed and we opted for the further
away, but safer, harbor of Everett.

The Shadowfax came with two headsails (jennies) one very
large, one smaller in size. The latter sail balances the whole
of the boat while underway, so the helm steers easily
without the overpowering sense that the steering wheel is in

control of the vessel (called weatherhelm). The larger sail overpowers the Shadowfax in higher gusts of wind, although for racing it might be ideal. With the smaller sail in place the Shadowfax seems more agile, able to turn deftly and point up wind at a better angle, leading me to remark that the boat felt more like a ballerina. Captain Bob gave me rather a quizzical glance at this remark since the Shadowfax is a hefty ballerina at 9 tons. My response was" Walt Disney did it with hippos!'

Have to admit the Shadowfax in a tutu is beyond even my imaginative skills.

Cape of Many Colors

May 4, 2008 Prevost Harbor, Stuart Island, Washington

This has been an extremely cold spring in the Pacific Northwest, with snow in April and from the looks of it, frost in May. Not a particularly encouraging time to plan a cruise to Alaska especially when Captain Bob is in denial about the impending temperatures. Hints about taking a down-filled sleeping bag as a preventative measure were ignored, so as we entered Prevost Harbor for our last night on United States soil, I knew this was my last chance to procure a warm covering from our cabin located in the bay. This covering turned out to be a knitted shawl (or baby blanket), purchased at some long ago forgotten garage sale, stored there for just such a chilly occasion. What a magnificent object, obviously crafted with great care: blindingly bright stripes of alternating green, pink, florescent orange, white and red knitted six inch bands adorned the blanket. The size was small enough to allow this creation to be cocooned around my shoulders, the warmth enveloping my upper body, with tag ends of pink, red and green blanket drooping like bat wings from my arms. Stylish I was not, but warm, yes!

Our cabin fronts on the beach, with one property line bounded by a small private grass airstrip that runs east to west. In the spring the runway grass is green, lush and makes appealing foraging for the deer of the island. With glorious sunshine, crisp air, and the potential for a marvelous sunset, it only seemed appropriate to walk down the half mile runway to enjoy the view of Mount Baker from the eastern end. As we trudged down the runway the colorful cape's "wings" billowed and flapped around my shoulders, an odd sight, but style didn't matter, just comfort.

Deer were on the runway in front of us, a lot of deer, nearly 30, busy chomping down an evening snack in the last rays of the sun. We walked with our backs to the setting sun, our eyes focused on the pastoral scene in front of us. The exhalations of the grazing creatures created white plumes in the cold air, matching our own breath as we marched steadily along. This foggy mist rose above us and the deer, swirling and forming a light ground fog in the still air, creating a surreal scene. Heads, some with budding antlers, rose as we approached, and we assumed the glazed look in the staring eyes was due to the vision- blinding sunset rays. Standing quietly, the deer were motionless, looking at us with dark, limpid eyes, jaws working ever so slightly chewing bits of fresh grass. We were able to get within feet of them, close enough to see saliva drooling from well filled mouths As we ambled past these grazing gourmands, strangely enough, we noticed the animals didn't bolt as we passed, heads just swiveled and the now intent, focused, no longer glazed, gazes continued. This process continued down the runway until we had 30 deer standing staring at us in perplexity. Then it occurred to me...the cape! Never before had these creatures been treated to such a visually stunning Technicolor spectacle, they didn't know what kind of creature I was with such a colorful hide and were overcome with curiosity; obviously something so ridiculous appearing didn't pose a threat. Local hunters must not be aware of this new deer attracting technique, or our woods would be filled with more of these garish capes during hunting season.

Don't let the secret out!

How Does My Garden Grow?

May 7, 2008 Cameron Bay , Nanaimo, British Columbia

The Shadowfax has a floating garden, of sorts. Sourdough starter (a yeast) is fermenting on a counter, and sprouts such as alfalfa, mung, and lentil await germination in the sprouting trays previously purchased from a survivalist source on the internet. This is to provide fresh salads from the sprouts; breads and pancakes from the sourdough. The sourdough batch has finally been tamed from repeatedly spilling, oozing, clinging, and smelly dough thanks to a recycled screw top coffee container that prevents all accidents. Tupperware and ziplock containers were no match for the sourdough on our previous voyage, allowing the batter to escape and dribble into ice chests, iceboxes and anywhere else it was stored. The resultant mess congealed into sourdough cement, some areas not cleanable until the Shadowfax returned to Meydenbauer Bay and home.

So far we have been able to purchase fruits and vegetables from the harbor grocery stores in Ganges and Nanaimo, but from this point on in our trip store availability will be less, and access to fresh food stuffs even more questionable. We do not plan to dock in Campbell River which is the next major supplier of foodstuffs in the Desolation Sound area. This will give us an excellent opportunity to sample all the varied dehydrated green beans, corn, peas , carrots, peppers, onions, potatoes, broccoli, and other produce on board. Of course we plan to supplement with the Cranberry

Coconut Macaroon Muffin Mix as necessary, with an ample contribution from Blueberry Muffin Mix as well. I suspicion the dried apples and bananas will do just fine in pies and banana bread.

The other item is short supply will be long, lingering showers such as provided in the excellent marina in Cameron Harbor. The Shadowfax has plenty of hot water and a warm shower when the engine is running, and a very cold shower when the engine is not. Water conservation and the temperature of the shower water have a definite shortening effect on shower length. To offset the brevity of showers, the Shadowfax has been loaded with a bountiful supply of body washes with fanciful names such as Mountain Spring, Arctic Force and Icy Blast each promising eight to twelve hour scent protection.

After the books I have read about the early inhabitants of the area, we have a life of luxury and safety on the Shadowfax. According to *Totem Poles and Tea,* and *Sitka Man*, twentieth century travelers were a much hardier bunch than we are today. They did without the equipment standard on our vessels such as VHF, GPS, radar and computer guidance. The young nurse whose story is told in the former book routinely traveled the open waters of Blackfish Sound enduring cold winter winds in a 15 foot open boat. The book is filled with recounts of a number of unlucky people, some tragically young, who perished attempting these trips. In addition to those illuminating texts, we have on board *North to the Arctic, Afloat in Time, High Slack, House Calls By Dogsled*, and *Ice Window*.

All of these books indicating I should have surreptitiously stowed the down sleeping bags on board.

Snow On Texada Island

May 11, 2008
Forward Harbor, Wellbore Channel, British Columbia

We have noticed the low snow level as we have slowly
motored and sailed our way north. White snow capped
areas of Texada Island in the Straits of Georgia and now
mountain tops have a dusting of fresh snow. This promises
to be a cold trip, but nothing like the trip of our redecessor,
Robert Kidd Watt, who traveled to Alaska in 1911 to look
for gold. He left a diary detailing his adventures and since
the book is starting to disintegrate from age, it seems
appropriate to transcribe it as we retrace part of his route
north. His sea journey brought him to Port Graham in Cook
Inlet (much further north than we plan to sail) and then
along the inlet to his goal of Beluga and the
commencement of his journey on foot.

The book is small with flaking pages, handwritten in pencil
with a terse, laconic style, brief to a fault, unless one
realizes the conditions he was writing under. The
Shadowfax provides electricity(solar and generated), heat,
shelter, radio and phone contact, internet access, a
computer, ample food, water and most of the amenities for
a comfortable life. I can type, revise, spell check, save,

print and do research at a desk, (the navigation station) and basically contemplate, write and rewrite for unlimited blocks of time.

Robert had to camp in rain, possibly snow, and write in spare moments when fingers were still agile, and time and light were available. The light must have been provided by candle, campfire light or kerosene lantern. Keeping a notebook and pencil dry must have been a challenge.

 The first days of the diary discuss a miserable boat ride up Cook Inlet, seasick comrades, long days and finally making camp. Hunting provided food, and the specialty at that time of year, duck mulligan, a stew of sorts, was accompanied by dried apple pie.I feel more of a kindred spirit with his companions, Martin and Jones; the diary doesn't clarify whether these are first or last names. They suffered seasick bouts on the sail up Cook Inlet and did not seem to be as well prepared mentally, or even physically, for the rigors of the trip as Robert. In his laconic style he mentions cutting a tree down to make a boat, unfortunately having the tree fall on top of the woodcutters. His comment in the following days: "Jones still feels bum", since Robert seems to be the master of understatement, I assume Jones sustained serious damage in the incident.

My Captain Bob, much like his grandfather Robert, is well prepared for our trip both mentally and physically, whereas I tend to fear and seasick bouts. The seasickness and fear occur at the same time in rough weather so I am never sure whether the fear comes first or the sickness. All I know is that at a certain point of wind velocity and wave height my comfort level is exceeded and I never know which orifice my stomach contents will choose to make their exit.

My comfort level is about 8 at the present time, which saves 9 and 10 for later, and truly nasty water.

Whiskey Gulf Invitational

May 12, 2008 Georgia Strait, British Columbia

The weather forecasts broadcast over our VHF radio makes for popular listening on the Shadowfax. We can gauge wind and sea conditions by listening to these automated voices that reportedly tell us what the weather conditions are like. Sometimes the forecasts are right, other times very wrong, but in those cases quickly corrected to match actual conditions.

One area mentioned in forecasts, having nothing to do with weather, lies in the Straits of Georgia near Nanaimo. "Whiskey Gulf" is a marine practice area for the Canadian Marine Forces, centered in the middle of the straits, blocking a direct travel route for north and south bound vessels. When Whiskey Gulf is "active" surface and subsurface torpedos are launched in practice making the area understandably hazardous. Mariners are warned over the calm, emotionless VHF broadcasts when they may safely transit this area. Otherwise the cryptic words," Whiskey Gulf is active today" means that mariners transit at their own peril, subject to vigorous warnings, and the potential of actual harm.

As we listened to the evening forecast for our upcoming day of travel we heard a new broadcast concerning Whisky Gulf activity. The area is not exactly closed, since there seems to be a marine party of Canadian, Australian and New Zealand forces doing a joint maneuver that allows for vessels to continue transit of the area without threat of damage or sinking. In listening to the report, it appears that the boat traveling public is invited to cross the area to order provide potential targets for these mock bombing runs. The broadcast is as follows:

"Area Whiskey Gulf will next be active May 13. North of Nanaimo area Whiskey Gulf as shown on Canadian Charts 3463 and 3512 will be open to mariners. However Whiskey Gulf will be over flown by long range low level patrol aircraft from Canada, Australia, and New Zealand Saturday May 10 through Monday May 12 dropping acoustical sensor devices and white smoke canisters."

Despite dire threats from torpedoes my comfort level is fine since I know the Shadowfax has no intention of trespassing in dangerous waters.

Snowy Amphitheatre

May 14, 2008

Blunden Harbor near Cape Caution, British Columbia

Our destination for the night's anchorage is Blunden Harbor, an old Indian settlement site complete with graves and longhouse ruins. This will be our last planned stop until we successfully traverse Cape Caution.

Of course, if the electrical gremlins have their way (yes, they are back!) we may not make it the 28 knots to the cape. Today a wire snapped off the alternator... the new alternator with practically new Balmer Voltage Regulator. As we motored into the Queen Charlotte Straits and had mentally decided to "go for it," Bob noticed that our engine was no longer charging. A quick dash below into the engine room confirmed the wire breakage, he made a quick repair and we were on our way once more. The lessons learned the hard way during our 2006 electrical training season have stayed with us.

Wind and tide cooperated and we were finally able to sail most of the way from Lagoon Cove to Blunden Harbor, a total of 45 knots in 8 ½ hours. I occupied myself with making ginger cookies which are reputed to alleviate seasickness. Unfortunately since we weren't suffering from that particular malady we had no reason to gobble up the fragrant goodies as "medicine. Darn!

While Captain Bob happily occupied himself with sailing and adjusting solar panels, I sat in the cockpit admiring the spectacular scenery. The rain of the last few days ended as soon as we sailed into Queen Charlotte Straits. The grey clouds suspended over snow coated mountain peaks thankfully hoarded their moisture for further inland away from the Shadowfax. As grey of the clouds merged into the grey of the water an illusion was formed: that the water and air were one, separated only by the dark blue strip of Vancouver Island mountain peaks that levitated and floated in the distance. These peaks formed a circular amphitheatre, blue crowned with white, with us, very small and insignificant at the center.

Evergreen trees on the shore, molded by strong storms, point away from the prevailing gusts; giant bonsai trees with fanciful bends and tops resembling flying saucers, the lower limbs having been shredded by the winds in previous tempests. Some trees simply jut straight up, limbless and needleless, just the trunk remaining as a skeleton to contrast with living neighbors, we are back in the land of" stick trees".

I Have A little Shadow

May 16, Fury Cove, British Columbia

There is an old children's nursery rhyme that goes" I have a little shadow that goes in and out with me". Every time we get into rougher seas this rhyme plays itself in my head as I watch the poor little Shadow being dragged along behind the Shadowfax led on its tether. Back and forth, up and down, the stoic Shadow grimly trails behind.

The Shadow, as rock and rolling as the dingy is, seems to do much better in suffering these sea conditions than I do. When we started from Blunden Harbor to cross Cape Caution, the wind was slightly to the stern of the Shadowfax and we were able to motor sail comfortably. By the time Cape Caution was reached the swells had increased, the wind decreased so as we slid into a trough the boom would shake, sails rattle, rigging clatter and the Shadowfax move from a gentle rocking sail to a bucking roll, moving from side to side then back to front.(Not very comfortable for my metallic back and hips).Captain Bob claimed the Shadow was doing just fine in these conditions and he appeared to be happy sailing with periodic adjustments to sail and trim, so I left the two riders and went below to brace myself in the aft cabin. Knees against the warm wall next to the engine, back against the side of the Shadowfax, wearing long johns, encased in blankets I shut my eyes and lay quietly waiting for one of three things to happen.

The Engine to stop and leave us to the mercy of the rocks of Cape Caution

The wind and tide to increase to such strength that we end up on the rocks of Cape Caution.

The promised westerly wind to arrive to sail us past the rocks of Cape Caution.

I could tell when the third option occurred as the Shadowfax steadied, heeled over and water sounds indicating motion, not submersion, came from the hull as it slid in increasing speed through the swells. We sailed from Cape Caution to Fury Cove with perfect 15 knot westerly wind, sunshine, and Captain Bob in sailing ecstasy.

The coast line in this region is rocky, rugged, and white from the spray created by the large waves smashing onshore. Swells would inundate the shore, reaching upwards to the tree line, exploding, a white slash of salty froth, then recede, leaving white cascades and waterfalls to pour down the cliffs. These waterfalls, fueled by the lakes of seawater in tide pools high above the tide line, would continue until the next surge. The resultant force of these downward streaming sea rivers trapped air, creating floating fields of creamy sea foam that the Shadowfax traversed to reach the calmer waters of Fury Cove.

Despite the dubious name, Fury Cove was tranquil and beautiful, ringed with white shell beaches accompanied by peek a boo views of the Queen Charlotte Straits to remind one of our good fortune to be in such a kind harbor.

The Three Clocks of the Shadowfax.

Sunday May 18, 2008 Hakai Pass, British Columbia

Time on the Shadowfax is measured by three clocks; one battery operated original to the boat, the other two hand wound ship's clocks, later additions. One complete with chime comes from Robert Watt (Senior), and the other from my grandfather from his beloved *Northern Cross*. Both winding keys are kept in the navigation station, but unfortunately neither clock has been wound on this trip yet. We have never managed to get either time or the ship bell chime to coordinate with reality, so the incorrect clocks remain unwound. It is easier to look for the correct hour on one clock, rather than guess on the best of three.

It seems incongruous that we have the clock from the *Northern Cross* on the Shadowfax, and we hail the ship from Stuart Island. The *Northern Cross*, after my grandfather's death and its subsequent sale, spent it's last days in adjoining Reid Harbor and still resides there, on the bottom, marked by our Garmin as a sunken wreak.

The beaches at Hakai Pass were as spectacularly beautiful this time as on our last visit in 2006. Caretakers were still in charge of the lodge at Pruth Bay and the black cat was still in residence. In 2006 it was a very lonesome, skinny cat called "Crab Bait ", in 2008 the caretakers have changed and so has the cat. Now called "Spook" the cat is well fed and aloof, the black pampered darling of the household. "Don't let my wife hear you call the cat *Crab Bait*, we were admonished."

View: Carving at Pruth Bay, Hakai Pass, BC

We wandered the white sand beaches with two new friends, Bonnie and Ron, who we first met at Lagoon Cove. The weather was sunny and warm, no need for coats and raingear, and also no sign of the Raven. They offered us hot dogs barbecued on the beach, and later Shadowfax homemade bread was shared. Our paths have intertwined until now, but their boat is larger, faster and so is their agenda. They have moved on ahead of the Shadowfax but perhaps we will see them again as we have the same final destination- Glacier Bay.

The raven did show up at Pruth Bay, just not on West Beach. A pair has set up housekeeping in the bay nearer to unsuspecting targets and their food. We watched as a huge bird flew to a neighboring boat's rail, hopped around on the cabin and checked out any potential food sources. We also had one of these magnificent creatures hop around on the Shadow at the caretaker's dock, but with nothing edible in view, the bird left. The birds only seem to like to STEAL food, when we made a birdie offering of hot dogs placed on a foil plate on the Shadowfax bow the treat stayed there until the next day. Although from the amount of droppings(poop) on the Shadowfax deck, one of the ravens had perched high in the rigging for some time contemplating whether it was safe to retrieve such a luscious prize.

  We made it too easy for them; perhaps a black garbage bag
hidden under Shadow's seat would have seemed a more likely
source.

Shadowfax Deploys a Drogue

Saturday May 24, 2008 McKay Reach, British Columbia

We must be mindful of the fact the Shadowfax is temperamental, and will misbehave if her crew behaves in less than nautical fashion, and this crew includes the dingy, Shadow. The winds were stronger than we anticipated when we left a calm Butedale this morning. Looking down the channel, it was evident that wind speeds were going to be impressive as spray from waves turned into swirling tornadoes of white ahead of us. Wind gusts heeled the Shadowfax over to 20 degrees, the ship reaching speeds of 9 knots with just one reefed sail, unfortunately this velocity combined with a few wind gusts of 40 gave the Shadow, our dingy, the ability to become airborne as it was towed along behind the larger vessel. First the dingy flipped into the air, bounced upside down on the waves, next a gust of wind flipped the dingy upright again and it appeared to twirl, air bound, on its mooring line until the disgusted Shadowfax put an end to this kiting activity by scuttling it. Kite flying is not a nautical behavior.

A drogue is a water filled sea anchor, and that is what the Shadow became, dragging behind the Shadowfax sometimes right side up, filled with water, or upside down, minus water. It successfully performed its function of slowing the larger craft down to five knots until we entered calmer water, smaller waves and managed to anchor. It would have been too dangerous and difficult to rescue the dingy in such conditions. These winds seem to be always hitting us "on the nose" this trip which means slow going and very little sailing. The wind gusts follow the channels with much stronger venturi effects between mountainous peaks, following shoreline contours, and as we round points of land, meeting winds from both in front and behind.

Our anchorage this evening is marginal, with wind gusts of 10 or higher in the "bay". We are in Coghlan Anchorage near Hartley Bay and our next goal of Grenville Channel which leads to Prince Rupert.

My comfort level on this jaunt was not good; I'd give it an 11 on a scale of 1 to 10.

Bear Attack at Butedale

May 26, 2008 Kxneal Harbor, British Columbia

Our next transit up Grenville Channel has been uneventful, except for the scenery. The sun has been out, the current with us, the Shadow dutifully towing behind right side up. Two years ago when we traveled this way, it was raining and the mountains hidden from view, now they shine with white and snowmelt is pouring down all the hillsides. We have seen a few ski slopes begging to be skied, including one that duplicates the features of Crystal Mountain's Silver Queen Run. As we exited Kxneal Harbor at 7 AM to finish the transit of Grenville Channel, the water was so still that the Shadowfax appeared to glide upon the snowy reflections of the mountain peaks.

Butedale was also sunny, but windy, forcing us to spend an unexpected night there two days ago. The ruins of Butedale are much the same as our last visit here, only more ruined. The old bunkhouse standing two years ago partially collapsed last February from the weight of three feet of heavy snow, and the rest of the building promises to join it soon. The caretaker, Lou, was still there as was his dog, new cat and a carefully tended heart-shaped garden. The garden was sprouting some lupines and columbines, an event that promise colorful flowers later in the season. Bert, the dog, is of medium size, indeterminate age, dark, very hairy, and totally devoted to Lou. We asked Lou about the white" spirit" bears and he said they should be out of hibernation but he hadn't seen one yet. The black bears were out and Lou even told a story about four grizzlies in the area that tried to attack a hiker.

The weather was so beautiful Captain Bob and I decided to hike to the nearby lake to fish and perhaps catch a glimpse of these white bears, so we donned rain pants, boots and long sleeve shirts for the trip. What a hike! Mud and skunk cabbages covered the "trail" and we climbed over vertical tree roots and rocks to reach our goal, boots sucked down into muddy holes that seemed to be bottomless. By the time we had climbed halfway to the lake I was wishing I hadn't refused the bear spray offered by Lou for protection. The woods seemed impenetrable and possibly full of unseen wildlife.

We reached the lake after squelching through bright red moss filled with snowmelt, the "trail" easy to follow since it was so muddy. Captain Bob scrambled out on the floating logs covering the end of the lake to fish, and I sat on a large log by the shore basking in the sun. It was quiet except for the sound of water and a few bird calls. I was almost asleep when I heard rustling in the huckleberry bushes on the small hill above me. As I turned my head to face the noise I saw a small bear running straight for me. I yelled in shock thinking my mauling was imminent, when I realized the bear was really Bert, the dog. He and Lou had followed us up to the lake to "protect" us from bears and join the fishing party. Lou was carrying an axe which he used to enthusiastically whack at brush and trees on the trail, and provide some protection from predators, perhaps.

Bert wasn't interested in bears, he just wanted to hop into the lake and cool off his tummy after the hot hike. He didn't stay in the water long, however, choosing to follow his master walking on the many logs that littered the lake. Bert never left Lou's side, <u>ever</u>. As the three of us headed back down to Butedale, Bert would travel in the middle of our group of hikers until he felt perhaps Lou was too far behind, then, he stopped and waited, tripping whoever was unfortunate to be directly behind him.

Lou has become quite an artist, crafting yellow cedar carvings and wood painting. These items are offered for sale, and we purchased a wooden "postcard" with his rendition of the Butedale ruins eloquently featured on its front.

Porpoise Playmates

June 7, 2008
Stephens Passage, 28 miles from Juneau. Alaska

Yesterday as we proceeded up Frederick Sound into Stephens Passage the Shadowfax found some porpoise playmates. About 15 or 20 of the black and white version discovered us and spent about an hour gamboling near us, they leapt in front of the bow and tumbled directly under us as we motor sailed. The speed wasn't enough for a bow wake, but seemed perfect for them to play tag and" keep away "with the Shadowfax. There seemed to be a game where two teams of porpoise would build up speed at the stern of the boat, becoming torpedoes with water mounded up over their bodies as they headed explosively for the Shadowfax' bow. These "teams" would pass each other nose to nose just under our anchor where it lay suspended over the front of our boat. We listened to the forceful exhalations of their breaths as they prepared to dive, and could clearly see their black and white markings as they swirled under and down underneath us. This game was repeated over and over again, with such high reaching splashes that the radar screen registered a halo around the boat.

 Perhaps they appreciated the sleek streamlined sides of the Shadowfax and used it for a convenient back scratcher or perhaps we were the only vessel providing moving entertainment at the time.

Gremlins Return

June 8, 2008   Windham Bay, Alaska

As we have traveled these waters I have entertained myself by reading such frigid material as *Frozen in Time, North to the Night, The Klondike Fever, The Ice Master and Robert Kidd Watt's 1911 Diary*, all books concerning arctic conditions and survival. Death, starvation, frostbite, danger, cold and simply miserable conditions all caused by the inflexible winters of Alaska and places further north. The books discuss blackened flesh on hands and faces, amputation of gangrenous limbs, frozen hair, tattered beards.

Not very encouraging, my comfort level floats between 8 or 9.

Unfortunately the gremlins on the Shadowfax have been reading these books too, and have decided to sabotage our diesel heater so we can experiment with those same conditions. The diesel heater stopped running this morning and a reset of the breaker and a new glow plug didn't produce any improvement or change in heat production. The expensive rebuild performed on the unit two years ago has only lasted long enough to get us <u>back</u> to Alaska.

View: Petersburg looking towards Thomas Bay

 Guess we head for Glacier Bay wrapped in coats, gloves and boots.(I KNEW I needed to bring those down sleeping bags!) Captain Bob optimistically commented, "Well it can't be cold all summer" Ha!

As I type this the sun is out, the temperature outside is 53, so we are not in too bad a condition. Nothing like the 40 below zero temperature registered on thermometers with ice encrusted boat decks and rigging mentioned in some of these books. Hoonah , located a bit north of Juneau reported a crisp 31 degrees this morning, and since we are heading that way I have to assume we may have some frost on the Shadowfax.

We entered the inner body of Windham Bay to spend a second night and to find the gold that prospectors might have overlooked at an abandoned gold mine. Eagles abounded, adorning trees, walking on the mudflats, circling in the air above. The question of what the eagles were munching on was answered as we anchored and saw trout jumping. We watched as eagle squadrons flew "bombing runs" with the twist that they were picking up, not dropping, attempting to catch a fishy meal.

Shadow took us up the mouth of the river a short way until it got too shallow then Captain Bob tried futile rowing against the current, an attempt soon aborted. The Shadow ended up beached on the gravel bar, and we spent a pleasant hour combing the beach for treasure, waiting for the tide to come in.

We found gold, the fool's kind, but the gravelly river bed trail was a welcome walk so we didn't mind too much.

Of Cruise Ships and Helicopters

June 11. 2008 Auke Bay, Juneau Alaska

Juneau gave the crew of the Shadowfax the opportunity to sample sightseeing with a cruise ship flavor. Five mammoth vessels had arrived in the harbor and passengers were busily taking advantage of the shopping and sights of this retired gold mining town. We purchased bus tickets at the cruise ship docks in order to tour Mendenhall Glacier, and then were whisked away on a bus, painted white to disguise its school bus origins, meanwhile treated to a detailed description by the driver of the sights we were charging past. The bus reached the glacier, perfectly on schedule, parked next to a number of other buses and disgorged its load of tourists, ourselves included. We dutifully hiked the short distance to the lake at the base of the glacier, observed the icebergs brought up to the Park Exhibition Area for display and smiled appreciatively on cue for the ranger giving her endless explanations of "blue ice". When one batch of tourists finished listening and moved on, the spiel was restarted with the same enthusiasm and inflections as before for the next group.

We tramped with our group along the trails to the waterfall and truly it was a sight to enjoy, despite the cruise ship flavor. Dry gravel streambeds under our feet attested to the massive spring runoff and melt earlier in the season. Five hundred feet above the falls three specks of white turned out to be mountain goats, a mother and two babies grazing despite the ruckus of the tourists pointing from below and the helicopters flying above.

Helicopters, dispatched from cruise ship terminals provide approximately 20,000 landings per year on the glacier, according to some data I gleaned from a permit site. The noisy machines are limited to only half of the requested landings per year due to the fear that they will disrupt ice, eagles, mountain goats, bears and most importantly, local residents. As we stood below the waterfall looking up, the helicopters hovered and swooped, giant dragonflies flying in droning formation, propeller noise echoing in the basin of the glacier, a "whack, whack, and whack". How the mountain goat could ignore all the hubbub was amazing, unless it was a tame goat, tethered out as part of the park exhibit, used to the noise and carefully brought into a stall in the evenings. I suggested this theory to a lady standing next to me and she was amazed at the concept, but gullibly willing to believe the parks department had fabricated this nativity style view for the cruise ship tourists' entertainment.

The question most often asked by all these tourists is "What ship are you on?"? We answered with "Shadowfax", the answer creating puzzled looks on the faces of people waiting to hear "princess this" or "star that'. I assume there must be a hierarchy of boat status associated with amenities and ages of the huge vessels. They couldn't place us either through attire or boat name.

As we left the park and its iceberg exhibition area, a different ranger was giving the "blue ice" spiel. The miniature ice bergs posed on display were slightly more melted, and the ranger, an aging Pippy Longstockings, had impossibly long red braids, but the recitation was the same, produced with smiling cheer.

Black Cats And Shadowfax

June 15, 2008 Hoonah, Alaska

The Shadowfax seems to have an affinity for black cats, first "Crab Bait"(later renamed "Spook") at Pruth Bay, now 'Salem" the dock cat of Hoonah. "Salem" hopped aboard as soon as we tied up to the marina's dock and proceeded to wander through the interior and over the exterior of Shadowfax rubbing against stays, hatches, even Shadow's sides were included. The cat traipsed in and out at will, meowing for a petting and tail scratch with which we were happy to oblige. He sprawled out on all the scattered rugs, rather like Goldilocks at the three bear's house, attempting to find the perfect spot. The best spot turned out to be our bunk, but when Captain Bob stared hard at him he quickly moved off the chosen site and opted for a safer place on the galley rug. We had to evict an unwilling "Salem" at bedtime, and for the remainder of the night could hear his kitty footfalls on the deck of the Shadowfax trying to gain admittance.

"Salem's" owner warned us that he had a habit of stowing away on unwary boater's vessels, necessitating a return to harbor and we were warned to check the Shadowfax out well before leaving. While 'Salem" is a perfectly behaved cat at the dock, under power or sail at sea he turns into a maniacal beast better returned to Hoonah as soon as possible.

Hoonah is a small village whose ravens and eagles far outnumber its residents. The entry pathway to the harbor passes a funerary island with sagging crosses and concrete burial boxes of its Tlingit founders. The statues of the cemetery turned out to be roosting eagles, using the solitude of the island for a respite from live human intervention. Ravens appeared tame, indicating that the people of Hoonah accept and welcome these black scavengers. In the witchcraft mentality of the white culture, crows and ravens are hated, feared and often shot at with intent to kill or chase off.

Not in Hoonah.

Requiem For a Purple Fleece Bathrobe

June 16, 2008 Glacier Bay, Alaska

> *O Purple Fleece who succored me*
> *Through surgery and misery,*
> *I lay to rest your comforting folds*
> *And hope to replace you ere the weather*
> *turns cold.*

One of my clothing comfort items is no more, inadvertently melted in an over zealous dryer in Hoonah. My purple fleece bathrobe that cloaked and comforted me through three major hip and back operations no longer has the right feel, its fibers congealed by a high heat setting that melted the softness into brillo. I feel as lost as a child without the special protective " blankie" that is a succor in times of stress. I debated the virtue of cutting the ruined garment into pieces to see if a small softened area would form the same bond-comfort as the original enveloping robe did. Reasonability won out, part of the allure of the robe was its all encompassment, a part of the original would never provide the warmth and seclusion of the whole, so into the oil rag bag it goes, perhaps. Like an addict I still need to be able to view the *purpleness* that masks the harsh feel of its fabric, so it is rolled up in a ball in the locker, preserved in its entirety. Perhaps I will pull it out and hold it when my comfort level goes over 6. It <u>will</u> be over 6 in the next few days as we travel through Glacier Bay, due to my fear of whales, icebergs and catastrophic "Titanic" style collisions.

Rather like our ride on the Hawaiian ferry from Molakai to Maui when barf bags were passed out prior to rough seas, I am anticipating the worst.

The security force at Glacier Bay might be the greatest threat. Reservations are required to enter this great national park, and it is mandatory to radio the forest service prior to exact entry of its hallowed waters. Timing is essential, so Captain Bob bolted out of bed this morning at 2:30 AM to catch the morning ebb tide for Glacier Bay, we left Hoonah at 3:00 AM. It was light even at this hour, and we were enthralled with the spectacle of feeding leviathans, humpback whales, with an entourage of sea lions, sea otters and eagles, out in number, all catching breakfast. As we reached the contact point at 8 AM and radioed in our permit number we were given clearance to proceed and instructed to report for a 1/2 hour orientation session. The Shadowfax was to travel directly in the middle of the channel, staying at least one mile from any shore, until Bartlett Cove and the park headquarters was reached, then the approach the dock was to be made at a 90 degree angle. This smacks of the USA Homeland Security Department, and I wonder what happens to vessels that don't comply, or even approach at the wrong angle. I suspect they either garner a hefty fine and incarceration, or perhaps an expeditious torpedoing for the watery infraction. The security level at the forest ranger dock was listed as MARSEC 1, this curious abbreviation for some governmental technical speech, means that by entering these waters you agree to be inspected and/or searched. Have the floorboards ripped out? Fingerprinted? To underscore this governmental power we were met on the dock by a very nice, uniformed, complete with gun-in-holster-ranger, who obviously was hired for his good looks, tall stature and fitness.

A potential search didn't seem so ominous any more.

Hazards of Glacier Bay

June 19, 2008 Reid Inlet, Glacier Bay Alaska

Of all the disasters that could cause the Shadowfax trouble, a cruise ship wake was not on the potential list. The National Forest Service has so many rules and regulations to protect wildlife both on land and at sea in the park that it never occurred to us to suspect the speed of the behemoth cruise ships would not correspondingly show some restrictions. Evidently not or perhaps the captain was so thrilled with the sunny clear weather that he forged ahead full steam in order to squeak out every bit of sightseeing for his passengers. At any rate, the Shadowfax was slammed broadside with a volley of sharp six foot waves throwing me out of a bunk onto the floorboards (on my back, of course),breaking teapots, ejecting cabinet contents and knocking all items not storm- stowed to the floor. We could see the havoc the waves created along the shoreline behind us, ricocheting back and forth along the rocky beaches, roiling breakers hitting high on shore. The seal and sea otter population that the parks service is desperately trying to protect certainly were tumbled around from these miniature tidal waves, so it surprising there is not a no-wake or small-wake zone in Glacier Bay waters. Later over the VHF we overheard two cruise ship captains discussing bearings, headings and visuals, one captain asking for location information from the others. The response of one captain to the inquirer was: "Can't you get a visual?" Now that is scary, three vessels each the size of a high rise building not being sure about the direction of their courses

either by compass or sight! First the S***dahm asking the
V**dahm, then the W***terdahm hailing the S***dahm .
(The names have been obscured to protect the innocent)

We traveled up from the mouth of Glacier Bay about 40 nautical
miles of distance, that's a day and a half of travel, Shadowfax
cruising speed. As we motored in a northerly direction into the
vast bay, the shoreline vegetation changed from evergreen
forested slopes to alpine meadow within these miles. Bushy
scrub, deciduous black cottonwood trees and huckleberry bushes
predominate with a scattering of darker Sitka spruce, Christmas
Tree perfect in form, all growing with persistent tenacity in
these spartan conditions. Looking ahead milky blue glacial
waters blend into greener steep slopes, an almost imperceptible
transitioning to sculpted ice of mountain tops, the spectacle
reaching as far into the distance as vision is possible, rising
thousands of feet straight up. Rivers of white and blue ice, their
rapids forever frozen in place appeared to stream down to sea
level, chunks falling off precipitously and transforming into
icebergs that floated not so silently away, with gunshot loud
sound effects as they broke off.

One of these iceberg producing rivers will head our anchorage
tonight, providing a glacial bowling opportunity with a tethered
Shadowfax as the kingpin. As we prepared to anchor our vessel
in this bowling arena, the wind picked up with gusts heeling us
over and churning whitecaps up to snap at our hull. The guide
book said to beware the strong afternoon and evening wind

flows, caused by air funneling through mountain valleys, buffeting the westerly exposed harbors with a venturi effect, and would pummel any vessels anchored within.

We heeded the warning and slunk off to another less windy spot. Captain Bob was extremely disappointed as he had already picked out the perfect martini ice to procure from the tidewater glacier on the shore.

Sasquatch Footprints

June 17, 2008 Russell Island, Glacier Bay, Alaska

After our aborted anchorage attempt in Reid Inlet we traveled across the channel to a moorage at the base of yet another mountainous amphitheatre, this one worn down with glacial snout out of sight. Anchoring at the appropriate "safe" spot suggested by our guidebook, Captain Bob plonked the outboard on Shadow and we headed to the far beach that was created of silt, sand and gravel from a glacial outpouring. The Shadow grounded, we waded ashore in milky waters, tied a long rope to the dingy so it couldn't escape and went for a walk.

The beach was a vast moonscape of rock and sand fanning out two miles wide by one mile long from a gigantic "gutter" at the base of the mountains. Its graveled sides must have been 200 feet high, and attested to the strength of the spring snow melt that spews from the 4,000 foot peaks sprawled over it. The gutter forms a maw and the fan of gravel a vast protruding tongue, perhaps the inspiration for Tlingit masks with their grimacing mouths and menacing features.

The sense of vastness is overwhelming in these vistas, it is no longer possible to judge distances in this land, the scale has changed to something we have no way of calibrating.

An estimate of one mile in distance could in actuality turn out to be two or three or even more miles, a small boulder viewed on the shore turn into a house sized hulk when visited in proximity.

Wandering this beachscape, in amongst the rocks and gravel were sandy pathways, and clearly imbedded were footprints, eerily humanoid, and in scale with the rest of the scene, immense. The prints were deep, wide with rounded five toe marks pointed ahead of the ball and heel of the foot, also there were more than <u>one</u> of these creatures, as the prints varied in size and depth, therefore weight of the creature. We assumed it must be a family, coven, pack or whatever one calls a group of unknown creatures who scurry with seeming purpose along the beach. Some tracks in the pathway appeared to be proper bear prints, causing Captain Bob to joke "It must be a Sasquatch with a pet bear on a leash".

This may not be so far from the truth as the shrub Myrica Gale on page 81 of the *Plants of the Pacific Northwest Coast* is mentioned as "Monkey Bush" in the Stl'atl'imx tongue because it apparently was used for some purpose by sasquatches. They believed in the validity of sasquatches. There was plenty of Myrica Gale at Mendenhall Glacier, and I assume it would thrive at the base of these glaciers, also.

Perhaps we just missed a party of sasquatches out for an herb-seeking stroll on a warm sunny summer day

Hunt For The Perfect Iceberg

June 18, 2008 Tarr Inlet, Glacier Bay, Alaska

In keeping with the immensity of the Alaskan wilderness, the icebergs too can confuse with proper size estimation. We decided to restock our ice chest with iceberg ice, easily available in the waters of Glacier Bay. The issue was size, even the tiniest berglets cautiously crept up upon would surprise with unexpected heft, impossibly heavy to capture and hoist to the deck of the Shadowfax by the use of the fishing net. Mind you, this fishing net is not puny; it is substantial enough to haul in a 20-25 pound thrashing halibut.

 As Captain Bob stationed himself in a pickup position on the bow, the Shadowfax was carefully nosed in for the capture, the scoop was made, with the first two attempts ending in failure with bergs either too big for the net or too heavy to lift aboard. Captain Bob would snag the ice and tow it along in the net beside the hull of the boat before a decision was made to keep the catch, or release it. The Shadowfax was very patent with our antics, although it would have been amazingly easy to drop Captain Bob over the side with some of these gyrations.

It must have been because he was wearing a life jacket.

John Muir
June 21, 2008 Elfin Cove, Alaska

The first sentence in John Muir's *Travels to Alaska* filled me with admiration. Here is a writer who didn't give in to the literary repairs suggested by their publisher. His first sentence is lengthy, paragraph long, and like an aria sung by a buxom opera diva, filled with tension as to when either a breath is to be taken, or the ending arrives.

"After eleven years of study and exploration in the Sierra Nevada of California and the mountain-ranges of the Great Basin, studying in particular their glaciers, forests and wild life, above all their ancient glaciers and the influence they exerted in sculpturing the rocks over which they passed with tremendous pressure, making new landscapes, scenery, and beauty which so mysteriously influence every human being, and to some extent all life, I was anxious to gain some knowledge of the regions to the northward, about Puget Sound and Alaska. "   *John Muir*

He was a preservationist, geologist, botanist and philosopher whose name is displayed in Glacier Bay Park on some of the world's most spectacular scenery and whose influence with two United States presidents helped to create this wilderness area. He was an eccentric, known for brutal hiking at all hours of day or night, and apparently must have been somewhat of a pyromaniac, noting the 30-40 foot flames at his campfire near Wrangell, the glow of which alarmed town residents not used to such nocturnal goings on. If he had written his works in the 1960's and early 1970's he would have been suspected of using hallucinogenic drugs from his descriptions of the elation he obtained from the nature around him. He was a Naturholic.

Leaving Glacier Bay and John Muir's legacy, we headed for Elfin Cove, a well protected, albeit circuitous harbor that faces across Icy Strait and provides an excellent view of Taylor Harbor's tidewater glacier. Our moorage at the public floats provided the Shadowfax with the company of a larger sailing vessel that was a younger, more expensive version. It was a Swan with the same teak decks, white hull, blue trim and interior teak of our own Shadowfax, but with an additional 13 feet of length it was a much larger, luxurious sister. The three man crew, (flown by plane up from California), were long time sailors, racers and told of famous acquaintances, travels and crossings, as they welcomed us aboard for a grand tour. We were honored that they admired our own Shadowfax for its similar design, ignoring her slightly less noble pedigree.

We have had quite a bit of admiration this voyage when people notice we have sailed her from Washington State. The low, racy profile that nestles into the water creates an unexpected ruggedness and stability in these Alaskan waters with their sometimes violent winds and tides. That she is also capable of single handed sailing appeals to some austere sailors, who relish the privacy of lone crossings without the necessity of a crew. Fuel economy is also a consideration with diesel selling at over five dollars a gallon, filling a thirty five gallon tank is less painful than a five hundred gallon tank, making the Shadowfax most attractive to budget minded travelers.

Serenaded By A Master

June 21, 2008 Elfin Cove, Alaska

Internet and phone access were especially good in Elfin Cove, and as a result the phone call made to it's supposed "harbor master" turned into a 45 minute conversation about his life, and gave me an irresistible urge to visit the gentleman bearing a fresh batch of ginger cookies. Roy Clement is an 89 year old retired Alaskan fisherman, prospector, musher and trapper living in a small cluttered house on the outskirts of the boardwalk. I obtained directions from the small grocery store and trudged my way on Elfin Cove's meandering wooden walkways, which are supported by 40 foot pilings, until I reached the dirt path, the stream and the old ramshackle house at the far end of the cove. It took a while for my knock to be answered, but I was ushered in with all the appearance of an old friend. My gifts of fresh cookies and some decaffeinated sugar free instant chai drink were an instant hit, I wasn't sure whether he would be able to have the sugar in the cookies, so I brought the second item just in case. Turned out both were welcome as sugar was allowed, but no caffeine.

We chatted for a while and as the seat I was offered was blocked in part by a guitar case, music came up in the conversation. Thankfully I didn't have my ukulele with me or it could have been extremely embarrassing for me, as Roy Clement is a master guitar player, and my musical skills are sadly lacking. His instrument was an old Gibson, a beautiful creation and when he picked it up to play for me it was with love in its handling.

What a private concert, what an honor! His voice was deep and had a flavor of Johnny Cash to its depth. What his fingers had lost with age, his voice had retained, and he sang and accompanied himself so beautifully it was hard to believe I was sitting in a little house in Elfin Cove with such a virtuoso.

I was truly serenaded. We did have a discussion about the "Golden Years" and what havoc time has wrought for him, illnesses, no more cigarettes, caffeine, about the lost of his beloved wife,(a wonderful cook), and the changes of modern technology, but we both agreed that the alternative, no old age, was worse.

 At least he still has an agile mind, his music and the tiny house perched over Elfin Cove.

The Lone Tentacle

June 24, 2008 Tenakee Springs, Alaska

The docks of Tenakee Springs on Chichagof Island are spacious and best of all, fairly empty, so it was easy for the Shadowfax to navigate the two breakwaters and slide into a spot. The town, itself, sprawls along the harbor with a dirt road, picturesque cottages and the usual exuberant vegetation of Alaska at this time of year. The plants are many of the same that we have in Washington but much larger, because of the steroid growing effect of the long days. Cabin roofs are metal, in varying colors, creating a patchwork quilt tapestry of color along the shore, and bicycles in different stages of decomposition are parked haphazardly at doorways, ready to provide economical transportation. The village "hot springs" promoted in our guide book turned out to be a tiny greenish concrete bunker with segregated soaking schedules for men and women, the hours carefully posted on a tattered sign. This is a rustic community with the feel of age and decay, rusting tools, overgrown weedy yards, houses with peeling paint and aging wood, all outnumbering the newer and larger houses being built on the hillside above.

After our walk, we returned to the Shadowfax and passed a fish cleaning station on the dock. It was clean of fishy gore except for a forlorn octopus tentacle lying dismembered under the stainless steel platform. The tentacle appeared to be making a last attempt at escape, extended in a hopeless reach down into the water through the holes in the planking. Plucked from the dock, the tentacle was so fresh it still had its sucking reflexes, and its tiny suction cups grasped at my fingers in an imitation of life.

As scuba divers we have seen these creatures in their native habitat, their gelatinous texture above water transformed into sinew and grace below coupled with the intelligence that makes in them such successful hunters. Our major interaction with an octopus came years ago diving at Patos Island, our underwater friend we named appropriately enough, "Patos Pattie." She, or more likely, he, lived in a cave fifty feet below the surface, and would welcome our visits with a handshake of eight foot long outreached tentacles, longer if stretched out. She was fascinated with our camera gear, and fondled it with great interest; our wet suits on the other hand, seemed to be disgusting in either temperature, feel, texture or taste and caused a quick reflexive jerk away if inadvertently brushed. Neither divers nor octopus felt threatened by each other, just a mutual fascination of the eight legged for the four legged and vice versa.

We would no more think of eating one than a dog lover would consider eating "Old Yeller".

The Puzzle Of Angoon

June 25, 2008 Angoon, Alaska

The loquacious guidebooks that we have so diligently read and used are suspiciously silent in their descriptions of Angoon, perhaps in a transparent attempt to dissuade visitation. My history book notes that Angoon was a stronghold, a gathering place for a number of tribes that staged a major native uprising against Sitka in 1802. I wonder if the same resentment that created these attacks is still simmering, or if visitors are welcomed with the same cheerfulness we found in Juneau and Hoonah. We motored our way against the current into the inner harbor of Angoon and found a fuel dock, seaplane float, public moorage float and about fifty abandoned fishing boats in differing states of decomposition on the beaches. It was a marine cemetery comprised of the older wooden hulls gradually melting away with rot, and newer fiberglass hulks that remain permanently, festooned with seaweed garlands, the vessels all a monument to "Global Warming".

The residents didn't seem to hold any centuries old grudges, they cheerfully waved to us on our walk and even showed a concerned worry that we would encounter one of the many brown bears in the area. Perhaps they thought we might attempt a tourist trick to pet, feed or take a close up picture of one of these furry behemoths and get attacked.

The buildings that from a distance appeared to be metal cannery buildings, turned out instead to be the local elementary and high school buildings, and the graying houses on the dirt street fronting the town's main pier must mirror Mamalilicula's appearance a hundred years ago before its abandonment and resulting ruin.

A number of totems, covered with mildew and moss gazed towards the water with wistfulness, faded features still straining to view the bay. Bear, killer whale, raven, eagle, and shark, they once had been carefully crafted and painted, now sit alone with only weeds and satellite dishes for company.

The Red Mark On The Shore

June 29, 2008 Gut Bay, East Baranof Island, Alaska

Whales have provided much of our entertainment traveling through these waters, especially the interaction of some killer whales with a group of humpback whales. The ponderous humpbacks had positioned themselves next to a steep rocky shoreline as they moved along and seemed to be using it to buffer the killer whale antics of jumping, spy hopping, flailing and thrashing. Since the Shadowfax was approximately a mile or two away we had a good view of the event. One particular antic involved a killer whale lifting its head and upper torso out of the water and apparently "walking" on its tail, much as trained porpoise do in aquariums. We watched the humpbacks until out of sight, still trailing their uninvited orca whale harassers. Unfortunately we may have been witnessing an attack by transient killer whales on their larger cousins. (There were reports of orca attacks on humpbacks a few weeks later in the same vicinity.)

Our last two anchorages have been at the base of vertically aligned mountain peaks, snow melt water poring down every conceivable crack to foam into the inlets where we sit for the night. The currents from these rivulets, streams and rivers form such a strong current that the Shadowfax is always pointed towards their source, despite the wind and tides inundating the inlets from opposing directions. Looking upwards we can see blue ice, indicating year round glaciers and crevasses whose avalanches have fallen straight down the sheer cliffs below them into the bays at their bases, piling up snowy patches that allow Captain Bob to hack out ice hunks for the ice chest. Handy when there are no stores in the area that have ice, actually no stores at all.

Our anchoring in Gut Bay was inadvertent, we had planned to motor or sail further down the coast, but the tide, wind and ocean swells were against us and Captain Bob was faced with a mutiny. Either head for a secure anchorage or turn and go with the wind back to Red Bluff Bay or even retreat further to Kake and head south a different route. Faced with this firm ultimatum, Captain Bob decided to opt for the secure harbor of Gut Bay and wait for the next day's northerly wind prediction. As it turned out, it was a fortuitous decision, allowing us to explore a bay every bit as spectacular as Princess Louisa Inlet, and allowed Captain Bob to catch a 30 pound halibut.

The octopus tentacle was put to good use as halibut bait, carefully dissected to provide the most catching ability on a lead head worm. Captain Bob caught two smaller halibut previously with this delectable bait, and he used the last piece in Gut Bay. The shore in the bay was marked with a red mark which I surmised (with great imagination) was a faded pictograph indicating the spot to fish, as in Desolation Sound. Sure enough, when Captain Bob caught his halibut, it was in the center of the bay in front of the mark.

An Alaskan Fourth Of July

July 1, 2008 Craig, Alaska

Our initiation into the fireworks of Alaska came as we entered the harbor of Craig, and prepared to find slip 39. It was a tight and shallow fit for the Shadowfax, and in my lip chewing concentration I failed to notice that two fishing boats, one tied to the dock, the other dodging rapidly back and forth, were involved in a fireworks fight. Loud explosions and smoke swirled from the two vessels as they pelted each other with explosive devices. Cherry Bombs may have been the weapon of choice as large plumes of water were expelled into the air as the missiles went off in the salt water with large shotgun sound blasts. Of course we motored right into the middle of the fracas which only stopped when the police showed up.

These fishermen were lucky they didn't hit us in the enthusiasm of some of their volleys, the closest we came to being directly hit was in one of the three docking maneuvers required to find our assigned slip due to the fact that the numbers had faded to nothingness and all harbormaster helpers had taken cover from the barrage. I can only imagine the retribution that might have taken place if we <u>had</u> been hit; a vicious swipe with a boom, a spewing of smelly head contents, or even an anchor projectile viciously slammed into an unprotected hull by a furious Shadowfax. The possibilities were endless.

We spent two nights in Craig, enjoying the book store offerings, laundry facilities with their bottomless coin receptacles and even a prime rib dinner at Ruth Ann's Restaurant to celebrate Captain Bob's birthday. Ruth Ann seems to be quite the entrepreneur, with restaurant, hotel and fishing charter businesses. The restaurant décor was charming, sporting leopard napkins and bright rose floral adorned wallpaper; one large painting seemed to suggest an exotic, possibly naughty, history of the hotel, now restaurant and bar. No more firework fights occurred during our stay.

Our next dock moorage was at Hydaburg, a small Haida fishing community with worn facilities, but cordial welcome. We were sold shrimp, and advised to re-tie our vessel to the dock in a different spot, a good move it turned out, since it was the 4th of July and the original berth was well within reach of fireworks. The town appeared deserted and as we arrived we wondered if everyone had driven to Craig for the festivities, it turned out not to be the case as the whole town was at their community center in a city wide celebration. Barbecues were smoking, children were running around with fireworks, booths were set up, people were mingling, participating in games such as egg toss, and the ever present dogs were scrounging for handouts. At dark the Shadowfax was treated to a magnificent fireworks display, seemingly a competition between the two ends of town for the biggest, highest, loudest display. Red, blue, purple, white, green, sparkling, shooting, cascading and even the few duds, the show went on for hours, a production that would put even large towns to shame in comparison. The accompanying whoops and yells that marked a particularly spectacular explosion were repeated until 3AM.

Snoring Whales

(Sent to Latitudes and Attitudes Magazine and was accepted, but they went out of business before printing this, hopefully not due to my literary skill)

July 8, 2008 Charlie's Cove, Cordova Bay Alaska

We are thinking of renaming our guidebook's "Charlie Cove" to " Bedroom Bay" in honor of the sleeping leviathans that snooze there. After a jostling sail across Cordova Bay to the Barrier Islands we were pleased to find this tiny cove unoccupied (or so we thought) and anchored for the evening. It was late, so a quick snacking dinner and it was bedtime for the two sailors. Captain Bob, before he turned in noticed strange noises in the twilight and went out in the cockpit a number of times to investigate; a growling, burbling, bubbly noise emanating from below, definitely not the anchor chain dragging on the bottom. Giving up, still puzzled, he went to bed to join his snoozing partner. The partner didn't snooze too long, awakened by loud snoring, Captain Bob was almost given a gentle elbowing nudge to quiet the racket, when it became apparent the noise came from outside the Shadowfax; we had two snorers, one aboard and one below! It was a burbling long drawn out bubbly noise followed by a whooshing gasp and the sides of the Shadowfax did an excellent job of amplifying the sound, much as it did for the little seal pup two years ago. Crawling out into the cockpit we tried steaming lights, deck lights and flashlights in an attempt to view the perpetrator in the dim light, but without success. The noise at times seemed to emanate directly beneath the Shadowfax, bubbling noises slithering up from the depths; unseen bodies leaving swirls in the inky water near the hull and other times, lurking quietly in the kelp fronds near shore. We quietly sat in the darkness and watched and listened to come up with a reasonable explanation for this nocturnal behavior.

The Barrier Islands, where Charlie's Cove is located, form a perfect area for protection from currents and wind; there are myriads of tiny islets so close to each other that they form an infinite number of protected moorages and in this case, whale napping sites. The feeding humpback whales that were so entertaining for us on our way through Cordova Bay were just getting an evening snack prior to bed time, with us, in Charlie's Cove. They could doze beneath the surface, releasing gargantuan lungfuls of air as they surfaced for a fresh breath and subsided again. The shallow depths and rocky islets formed their cradle, allowing them to float safely in a contained space without fear of cruising ships or purse seiners interrupting their slumbers. This bubbling breathing was the source of our snoring, and the gentle currents of the islands moved the sleeping creatures closer, then farther from the Shadowfax without awakening the snoring sleepers.

The whales slept, we didn't.

Santa Claus Of The Inside Passage

July 12, 2008 Prince Rupert, British Columbia, CA

Travel from Nakat Harbor to Prince Rupert was uneventful and thankfully smooth, we moored at the Prince Rupert Yacht Club, dispensed some Shadowfax Ginger Cookies and went into town to shop and have dinner. The Pub/Restaurant we chose for victualing overlooked the harbor and due to the excellent food and beer was, from the appearance of the diners, obviously a favorite for local residents.

Our table bench adjoined another table and the friendly gentleman turned out to be no other than "Santa Claus", a white bearded loquacious gentleman who soon told us his secret identity. A genial British sign painter by day, at Christmas time he transforms into a helicopter Santa who travels up and down the Canadian waters to provide visits and presents for the children who occupy the various lighthouses up and down the coast. We were amazed to learn how many children enjoy these Christmas visits despite the stormy weather that occurs at this wintry time of year. The passengers need to be securely strapped into seats to prevent being thrown against the ceiling of the craft as the helicopter dodges gale winds and 60 foot waves that threaten engulfment and annihilation during their visits to these remote stations. Santa obviously needs his padding!

Our conversation began about the history of the area, and when our 'Santa" learned I had read a book about Ralph

Edwards, a BC pioneer and a personal friend of his, he became quite informative. The biographies and history books we have on board the Shadowfax have intertwined in an informative and interesting fashion with the inhabitants that still live along these coastal waterways, greatly increasing the enjoyment of our travels.

In Prince Rupert we browsed yet another few bookstores and came back with a number of finds, including a good dictionary, James Michener's *Alaska* and Barry Lopez' *Arctic Dreams*. They now crowd the cramped shelves of the Shadowfax along with *Ralph Edwards Of Lonesome Lake, O Rugged Land Of Gold,* and *Cooking With Sea Vegetables*, ready to pitch onto the floorboards during the next rowdy sail.

Before we left, the next day, we took a batch of Shadowfax Ginger Cookies and attempted to deliver it to our "Santa", he wasn't home, so the cookies were hung on the door with a note in the hopes that come next Christmas he will remember the Shadowfax with kindness.

Peregrinations Of The Shadowfax

July 14, 2008 Principe Channel, British Columbia

One of the purchases made at the Salvation Army store in Prince Rupert was a book, *Arctic Dreams* by Barry Lopez, an author whose use of words is extensive, too vast for the Compact Webster's Dictionary purchased at the same store. Words such as pagophylic(birds and mammals who are ice oriented), alcids(black and white pelagic birds such as Auks) , artiodactyls(referring to both antelope and hippopotami, perhaps dancing or graceful?) and fata morgana(?) are scientifically related, and not to be found in this abbreviated version. Peregrinate, a word, actually does exist in Microsoft Word's spell check and the little dictionary, in the book's context it described an action of a polar bear. I wasn't sure whether it referred to the animals shivering, pooping or breathing until the little dictionary finally coughed up a definition," to travel from place to place, journey travel". Other words used such as tenebrous(dark, gloomy), lambent(shining) and xeric(?) are thrown in the mix to keep a reader on guard, to add or detract to the meaning or just show off the author's vocabulary, I have no idea. It is educational to grab up the dictionary at every other page, but very distracting from grasping the core message of the tome. Other words he might have used would be tergiversation (shuffling) in describing the walk of a walrus, or tessellated (tiled) to identify a of sea ice layer. What about a hebdomadal (weekly) event?

The Shadowfax has peregrinated, or traveled, half the distance back down the coast from Glacier Bay. Principe Channel, part of the rougher Outer Passage, today has a light northwest chop allowing the Shadowfax a stately wing on wing sail down its length. Trees along this section attest to the strength of wintery gales; tall silvery trunks, wind stripped of bark and upper branches, stab upwards, standing out against the remaining green of lower boughs and scraggly brush, their weathered grey visage overwhelming any vestiges of foliar green. In the sunshine, in this part of the summer, this stretch of our journey is incandescent with light bouncing off waves, white beaches and rocky shorelines, sunscreen and hats, short sleeves, sun generated warmth and long days.

In addition to the north winds and sunshine that speeds our voyage, Captain Bob even caught two salmon trolling from the stern of the boat after the mainsail was dropped(the Shadowfax does not sail and fish).

Life is good, and the rough water endured off Dixon Entrance is just a memory.

Back to Snowy Peaks

July 16, 2008 Graham Reach, British Columbia

> *Mountains are cut out of cold blue ice*
> *Snow as a cloak, comfortable and nice,*
> *Misty and covered with swollen clouds*
> *The mountains lie in their private shrouds*

> *Poem by Jacquelyn Watt age 12(or so)*

This trip up the Inside Passage has been an educational voyage; using texts purchased from the bookstores in various harbors, I have been able to tutor myself in the geology that somehow missed sticking in my mind during all those long years in school, fascinated by mountains, but knowledgeable, no.

The Khutz Inlet, with it's horseflies of 2006, now seen through my more learned eyes of 2008 and the lessons learned in Glacier Bay, now appears to be the remnants of an old glacier. Looking up, snow still cloaks(the word the 12 year old Jacque used) the towering peaks of the 4000-5000 feet mountains that frame the inlet, hinting of long ago even vaster snowy grandeur. Using my imagination, the glacier that once covered this area can reappear a mile thick, its tremendous weight gouging and clawing deep into the rock substrata, the gravel of its moraine forming a tongue-like dam that held out seawater until the warming earth and glacial recession caused breaches and its inevitable dissolution. The fiord would have been a landlocked lake at first, fresh water heavy, so that it would totally freeze over in winter (such as many of the Alaskan inlets, like Windham and Gut Bay still do). This would have staved off total meltdown for a period, but the salty sea would have won out over time, and the water's freezing temperature raised until the inlet remained ice free most of the year. Would this breach have been gradual or sudden; would the moraine dam have given way at the top with the pressure of spring melt and a torrent of silty glacial mud spew out into the air above the channel below forming a cataract, or would the whole edge of the dam have softened and collapsed with a quiet groan outwards? I missed knowing the answer by 11,000 years.

If my supposition is correct, the rocks of the moraine still remain, in piles underwater, upper portions of this "dam" forming the half moon spit we anchor behind at the mouth of the inlet. The gravelly, narrow and shallow channel at the northerly portion, which we use to obtain entry to the inlet, would perhaps have once been the ingress and egress of the waters, probably with landlocked icebergs held captive there, until rising sea levels inundated the area. The tremendous contouring ability of these glacial behemoths is evident nearby at the tip of Mathieson Channel, where in a narrow channel a rounded gouge appears to be bored horizontality a few feet above the high tide mark. As if the glacier had a bowling ball and scored the granite as it grinded past, a perfectly cylindrical half.

Moaning and Groaning

July 17, 2008 Klemtu, British Columbia

The moaning noise woke me up at 3 AM this morning; it
was a low pitched groan that started with a whisper, slowly
built in intensity then died away completely. The sound
came from outside the Shadowfax, it wasn't a snoring
sleeper or whale; it was the wind. This harbor is close to
the outside waters; we have noticed this same phenomenon
near Dixon Entrance, Cape Caution and Icy Strait. Gusts of
wind swirl across the mountains that line these shores,
perhaps the gnarled tree snags at their summits contribute
to the sound with a wood string effect from branches held
taut against the breeze, hollow cores resonating. Eventually
the wind reaches the Shadowfax rigging and twirls a
halyard or two, snapping them against the mast as if to
check the sound, creating a rattling beat that shivers along
the Shadowfax and then, just as quickly as it comes,
dissipates. The wind is high, off the water, so no waves
rock the boat, just the eerie noise, repeated over and over
again as if to check and recheck the tonal quality of the
rigging.

This process is repeated until the listener waits, with suspense, in anticipation of the next moaning event. One can lie in the bunk, eyes open in the dark waiting for the next halyard beat to start, or get up, check the anchor, squint at the clouds in the moonlight, realize that sleep is no longer an option and that a hot cup of coffee sounds good.

It will be a long day and a long sail until we reach Bella Bella.

Rain In the Central Coast

July 21, 2008 Namu Harbor, British Columbia

The local people of Shearwater/Bella Bella made the comment that this summer had been particularly stormy and rainy in the area, and we are experiencing this weather phenomenon in its entirety. The sun seems to have vanished, and we are huddled in a tiny harbor in the vicinity of Namu, waiting out the wind, rain and fog. Not even weather reception makes its way into these rocky nooks, so it is up to us to guess when it is safe to pull the anchor and evade the rocks blocking our escape of this harbor. Not that it has been an unkind area to sit for a day or so, waves as well as communication are blocked, so our anchorage has been peaceful, if not boring. The books on board have been read, some re-read, including lengthy textbooks of history and geology, the knowledge hard to retain in my mind, the hope that repetition will achieve retention.

One of these books goes into great detail of the physiology of northern creatures such as walrus, seals, narwhals, humpbacks and polar bears. Most of the information is entertaining, but not overly useful in these warmer Inside Passage waters. After our snoring whale episode in the Barrier Islands, I studied the book again, to gain a greater understanding of whale behavior, and analyze the author's claim that only narwhals and sperm whales sleep on the surface, he needs to add humpback to his list. A whale behavior not mentioned or dissected in this book is an event called 'breaching". We are familiar with this phenomenon in the warmer Hawaiian waters where the great creatures jump out of the water and then crash back with magnificent splashes. Tour boats capitalize on this behavior, making big bucks by taking tourists on viewing sessions.

We left Namu after the storm was spent, rain stopped, the sun came out, and with the sun came whale sightings, first the sharp spout of white breath erupting from the water; viewed from a distance the steam could be a mirage of fog, but the shape is distinct and subject to regular repetition, so identification can be made. If a tail is raised out of the water at the start of a dive, or if the whale leaps into the air, back arched, water streaming down, there is no problem with identification. Whale!

As we motored towards Hakai Pass one of these breachings occurred, a full body event, head tail and all, completely out of the water, the distance making the spectacular lunge appear in slow motion. What must it be like to leap into the air from the supporting cradle of the sea, to feel the sun on a skin used to darkness and deep pressures? Does it tingle, feel warm, does the slap of the re-entry sting? The book didn't discuss this issue, I can only imagine that it might be a reverse of our diving into the whale's watery environment: the entry jolt, the sliding into a different atmosphere, a temperature and pressure change, a change in hearing, sight, then quickly back into the normalcy of either air or water, man or whale. Both must enjoy the exhilaration of entering a different environment, surviving, conquering it and returning to the familiarity of sounds and feel of one's own world.

Fish Jump Cove

July 24, 2008 Fish Egg Inlet, Fitzhugh Sound, British Columbia

Don't look for Fish Jump Cove on a chart, it won't be there, this is the Watt naming of a small cove in Fish Egg Inlet, near Joe's Bay. The Shadowfax anchored in the midst of a school of jumping fish, salmon or trout, we never decided because they were impossible to catch. We cast white buzz bombs, pink buzz bombs, white worm lead heads with delectable fishy bait, Captain Bob got his fly fishing pole and tried with different artificial lures, casting, trolling, all to no avail. They jumped into the air, they surfed along the surface, they waved fishy tails, they swirled in the water and made loud splashes, but bite on a lure they would not. The fishermen of the Shadowfax were a frustrated lot; the only thing we didn't try was a leap from the Shadowfax, a panther-like attack on our fishy tormentors.

We next decided to take the Shadow and explore Joe's Bay with its rapids and connection to Elizabeth Lagoon. The rapids were easy to find, we followed the foam floating on the water, created from the air mixing with tannin in the brackish salt water. The foam was thick, substantial appearing, the bubbles able to support the weight of other bubbles forming a six to eight inch thick carpet that the Shadow plowed through, pushing it ahead of the bow, until it piled up gunnel height, a miniature toy boat icebreaker in a giant's bubble bath. We left a trail through this cream colored sea, with balls of foam blowing in the wind; delicate, rounded spheres rolling past the Shadow as we motored slowly against the current until reaching the base of the outpouring. As we left, our trail filled in quickly with foam erasing our pathway, as if we had never pushed our way in, as if we had never been in Joe's Bay.

My comfort levels have been perfect in the last few days with all the fishing activity, a perfect score of 0.

Place Where Enemies Lie in Ambush, Near Village;
Lying Flat On
Side of Head

July 25, 2008
Miles Inlet, Queen Charlotte Sound, British Columbia

This is a sample of one of the Indian names replaced by early explorers to the area, mostly British. It was replaced by names such as Deserters Island, McLeod Island and Tommy Point. *Groaning Beaches* was replaced with Blunden Bay, *Place to Dance on Beach* by Burnett Bay, *Having Shelter At Hind End* to Kent Island, and *Looking Like Smoke* to by Storm Island. At least the latter name was not for an English lord or early surveyor, but most of the renaming eliminated much of the romance of the native descriptions.

We entered our anchorage for the evening through a narrow channel, rocky sides forming a constricted passageway, impenetrable without GPS, the overhanging scraggy trees making travel even more of a challenge. As we glided warily through those still waters, a petro glyph seemed apparent, facing outwards, somewhat of a fishy shape, a warning, perhaps a protective sign? It was hard to decipher or even decide if the shape was truly manmade.

Miles Inlet did not have an earlier name associated with it; if it did it would have been something like: *Place having Osprey That Catch Many Fish*, or *Having Old Growth Trees, Crying Loons, Complaining Eagles, Noisy Ducks and Jumping Herring.* It might also have been given the name of *Site Where Hungry Black Flies, Gnats and Mosquitoes Bite People, Especially Sailors.* We didn't go ashore to check to see if it resembled the place called *Broken Out In A Rash,* a point near Everett, Washington.

The next morning after a peaceful night without nocturnal winds in this secluded harbor we proceeded on our way southwards. The petro glyph that was apparent on the rocks as we entered the harbor the evening before had vanished, or perhaps it never was, a figment of my overactive imagination.

 Our motoring turned into sailing for our next destination of Blunden Harbor and we moved at a stately 5 knots down Ripple Passage. Our engineless progress did not go unnoticed, our first inkling of company was the noisy splash of two sea lions that surfaced next to the Shadow at our stern, the next a growing barking, growling, belching, farting and howling noise from a nearby island. It was a sea lion colony, a group of perhaps 30 or 40 of the noisy, writhing, probably smelly creatures all warning us not to intrude on their territory. Out of curiosity I returned some of their howls with my own, and got an immediate reciprocal response, a growling and barking even louder than before.

I wonder what I said in Sea Lion Language, I hope it was polite.

Hukilau At Sullivan Bay

July 28, 2008 Sullivan Bay, British Columbia

On page 104 of *Exploring Puget Sound and British Columbia,* by Stephen Hilson, a note was made that the native name (translation by Boas) for Sullivan Bay was "Having Man-Of-The-Ground"(i.e., a fabulous people) It still does.

Sullivan Bay is a floating village; a store, restaurant, laundry, post office, and fuel dock accompanied by well built houses, supported by cedar float logs(or more modern floats), all with a profusion of mussels and varying kinds of watery décor attached to their tide-line levels. The water is clear, and looking down through voids in the gently moving decking and pathways, one is reminded how transient this village is with the water swirling underneath, gently moving the mussels as they feed, perhaps with a fishy " big one" lurking below, staring back, the watched watching. Wooden sidewalks provide access to all the structures and are liberally adorned with creative signage regarding local directions, distances to far flung geographical locations and, more importantly, proximity to the dog poop deck. Propane tanks sport bucolic scenes and fanciful metal sculptures of water fowl squat on dockside front porches liberally adorned with planter boxes, their healthy cascades of red begonia, yellow dahlia and purple lobelia adding a final touch to the festive air. Sullivan Bay has a cheerful, deceptively indolent and very successful feel.

Our stay at Sullivan Bay was enlivened by an impromptu concert; a number of boaters with musical skills assembled for an evening of singing and dancing in the Hawaiian way. It started with my ukulele's gentle strumming at Sullivan "Square", and evolved into a full scaled sing-a-long complete with enthusiastic hula performances. The ukulele must have conferred with mother nature, the weather that had been cloudy, albeit dry, turned into warm sunshine with the first notes, and remained that way until sunset and the ukulele was packed away again on the Shadowfax.

The restaurant provided yummy" pupus" that complemented the potluck contributions of the mariners that attended the fest. It didn't seem to matter that the beat was off occasionally, the key not quite right sometimes, and words missed; the enthusiasm of the performers made it a rowdy success. Perhaps another year the Sullivan Bay Singers will materialize again, if weather and talent form the right alignment at the small square in the harbor.

.

Sea Monster On The Shore

July 31, 2008
Moore Bay, The Broughtons, British Columbia

Rain descended upon the Shadowfax after Sullivan Bay, we dodged gale and storm warning winds, but were unable to escape the rains; we collected five gallons in our rain collector overnight, great for our water supply, terrible for our spirits. The rain pounded down on our deck, filling the poor Shadow almost to the point of sinking; with the accompaniment of lightening and thunder this deluge seemed biblical.

Across the bay a rocky face glowered at us, a tide line grimace with staring eyes, sockets overhung by scraggly brushes, and a scowling mouth complete with lips drawn back in a permanent howl. This visage was so horribly compelling that I checked the chart book of native names of the area and found that it probably was the site called "Old Man" (Sea Monster). This face must have communicated an ominous message of doom and disaster to early travelers of these waters, hence the name.

Along the sound landslides have scored the mountains top to bottom; vegetation free, rocky, thousands of feet long in some places; boulders, dirt and mud spewed into the water at their bases. Some gashes were created naturally because the sheer cliffs cannot hold on to soil with such massive amounts of rain, others created by effects of the clear cutting (unrestrained logging) that still occurs in these areas. There are pictures and stories of the huge slide at Corson Creek where half a mountain slid eighty years ago, whether from logging practices or an act of nature, the scar remains.

Most of the mountains in this area show barren logged patches, and places that show growth in these decimated areas show the green of alder, not evergreen. Beaches store the debris of this timber harvesting, covering clam gardens with a choking cloak of branches and root balls. It shows the careless waste and callous treatment of the area by large lumber corporations, and a shocking disregard for their long range effects on the natural recourses of the area.

The ominous landscape, rain and lightning established my comfort level at 6, but it soon decreased with the cessation of rain and the promise of sunny weather.

The Four Cups of Tea

July 14, 2010 Soulsby Point Cove, British Columbia

This should feel like a secure anchorage tucked into these narrow, rock rimmed channels, but the trees belie the illusion of safety. Once evergreens, most are now grey barked skeleton trunks with branches and most foliage long gone from effects of savage storms off the water. We are close to the full fury of the Pacific Ocean near Queens Sound, as the vegetation exhibits, so the transitory comfort of sunshine through the plexiglass of our cockpit enclosure gives little emotional warmth. Sea wind hums a low tune through the rigging and grabs a halyard to toss and bang sporadically as it moves over the Shadowfax. That same wind riffles the surface of the tiny bay we are anchored in, ruffling feathers of the hidden ducks and loons whose poignant cries with their resonant echoes start our dog, Raleigh, barking.

 We are isolated, no ships, kayaks or planes disturb this place, and even the abandoned fisherman's cabin on the shore matches the rest of this weather ravaged site's atmosphere. A caricature of a dock hangs precariously from the shore, once useful, now like the cabin so damaged from years of wind, wave and tide to be merely another hazardous memento, with its associated feeling of pathos.

Captain Bob explored the cabin, climbing carefully inside the rickety structure. At one time it boasted a stove, ladder and sleeping loft but now the roof where the stovepipe protruded has been blown away and moss carpets the upper loft, the stove lies rusting quietly on the ground outside and mildewed and mouse torn mattresses lay stacked in abandoned piles. Some glass windows miraculously remained, but doors were missing as was the generator from its dilapidated shed. A note, still legible was written on an inside wall exhorting users to keep the house clean and to turn and air the mattresses.

Incongruous in this desolation were four white china tea cups neatly placed upside down on a shelf in the area that must once have been delegated for eating and cooking. They were neat and clean, looking as if they were just waiting for hot tea or coffee to be served in them. Fittingly Captain Bob left the cups there on the shelf, using his camera to provide a memento of this experience, rather than disturbing the last pieces of order left here.

The next time we come this way the cabin and cups will likely be gone, but they will disappear together. It seems fitting.

Non Nautical Tales

Guantanamo Bay or Bust

Seattle to Maui   January 2009

Captain Bob and First Mate Jacque started out our first vacation of the year with a number of inauspicious natural and not so natural events. On the day we chose to fly to Maui from Seattle, a date chosen with much deliberation six months in advance, Seattle was hit with yet another of a series of fierce winter storms. Snow and ice on roads, freeways and walkways made for a seriously treacherous journey in the early morning hours to the airport.

The inhabitants of the Greater Seattle area are paranoid about snow and ice, dusting of the "white stuff" on the roadways and schools are closed, cars abandoned in the middle of roads, businesses shut down and public transportation compromised. We were understandably concerned about the dire weather forecasts, and when our planned commercial taxi transport to the airport chickened out a day in advance of the snow, we coaxed a good friend into giving us a ride. This is the true test of friendship: getting up at 4 AM to navigate treacherous roadways and expose your vehicle to the potential danger of snow & ice-crazed drivers in Seattle. Only an intrepid friend of many years would even contemplate such a much appreciated favor , especially since his passengers were heading to a sunny, warm 28 degree destination, Celsius not Fahrenheit!

Our ride showed up at the proper time with his vehicle, which turned out to be a large "duel tired" pickup truck. The truck was majestically loaded and stacked with two outhouses and two 15 foot sections of large culvert pipe sticking straight out the back of the truck bed, the whole resembling a strange spacecraft powered with twin rocket thrusters.

Despite our fervent offers to substitute our vehicle for the heavily laden rig, our friend chose to drive his totally inappropriate vehicle to the airport. The vehicle was appropriate in that it had four wheel drive; but visually it was inappropriate to take to the airport with all the Homeland Security restrictions in place. (Color Orange- for elevated.) Apparently our friend wanted to test the stability of the truck in the snowy conditions that confronted us prior to making his delivery of goods later in the day.

Passengers are not allowed to take more than three ounce containers of liquid products packed in zip lock bags- quart size- no weapons, knives, guns or toenail clippers ;and here we arrive with an oversized load of culverts and outhouses towering above the cab of the truck.(Guantanamo Bay here we come!)We managed to pull up in front of the terminal without mishap in part due to the driving skill of our friend, but mainly due to the unwieldy and unexpected appearance of our rig. Drivers slowed their vehicles and allowed us to proceed in front of them to deposit passengers and suitcases at the Hawaiian Air Ticket Counter. Perhaps the oddly loaded truck, the rustic appearance of the driver (see picture), combined with the full length leopard skin fur coat worn by the passenger created the impression we were filming a scene from "The Beverly Hillbillies". No self respecting terrorist would dream of attracting the kind of attention our arrival created.

 Suspicion was allayed; our arrest by Homeland Security and subsequent trip to Guantanamo delayed for the time being.

And so another series of adventures for the crew of the Shadowfax has been documented, printed and celebrated. Our next voyage will be in 2013 when we once again head up the Inside Passage.

Wish us Bon Voyage!

Made in the USA
San Bernardino, CA
24 March 2016